DAYS THAT SHOOK THE WORLD

THE INVASION OF KUWAIT

AUGUST 2, 1990

Dr. John King

Raintree

Chicago, Illinois

DAYS THAT SHOOK THE WORLD

Assassination in Sarajevo
The Chernobyl Disaster
D-Day
The Dream of Martin Luther King
The Fall of the Berlin Wall
The Freeing of Nelson Mandela
Hiroshima

The Invasion of Kuwait
The Kennedy Assassination
The Moon Landing
Pearl Harbor
The Russian Revolution
Tiananmen Square
The Wall Street Crash

© 2004 Raintree
Published by Raintree, a division of Reed Elsevier Inc., Chicago, Illinois

For information, address the publisher:
Raintree, 100 N. LaSalle, Suite 1200, Chicago, IL 60602

Library of Congress Cataloging-in-Publication Data

King, John, 1939-
The invasion of Kuwait / John King.
v. cm. -- (Days that shook the world)
Includes bibliographical references and index.
Contents: Tension in the Gulf -- Iraq: a menacing neighbor -- Kuwait: wealthy but threatened -- The oil-rich Middle East -- The Iran-Iraq War-- Between two wars -- Warning signs -- August 2, 1990: the invasion begins -- August 2, 1990: the first day -- The first month -- Theinternational response -- The prelude to war -- The war in the air --The oil disaster -- The aftermath -- The Arab world and the Gulf War -- Iraq since the Gulf War -- The Middle East since the Gulf War -- -- The world and Iraq.
ISBN 0-7398-6644-3
1. Persian Gulf War, 1991--Juvenile literature. [1. Persian Gulf War, 1991.] I. Title. II. Series.
DS79.72.K563 2004
956.7044'2--dc21

2003010109

Cover picture: Iraqi troops chant pro-Saddam and anti-American slogans as they prepare for the invasion of Kuwait.

Title page picture: Oil wells that were set ablaze by the Iraqi army as it retreated from Kuwait.

We are grateful to the following for permission to reproduce photographs:
Associated Press 11 (Gustavo Ferrari), 15 top (Amr Nabil), 19 bottom (Marcy Nighswander), 30 (Dominique Mollard), 43 (Laura Ranch), 31 top (Jon Swain); Corbis *front cover* (David Turnley), 9 (Nik Wheeler), 19 top (David Turnley), 24 (Ed Bailey), 26 (Susan Biddle); Corbis Sygma 43 bottom (Gyori Antoine); Popperfoto 8 (Reuters), 20 (AFP), 28 (AFP/Ruetshi), 29 (AFP), 31 bottom (AFP/Mike Nelson), 35 (AFP), 37 (AFP), 40 (Reuters), 42; Rex Features 6 (Sipa), 7 bottom Kol Al Arad), 16 (Fouad Matar/Sipa), 21 (Sipa), 22 (Wesley Bocxe), 25, 27 (Sipa), 38 (Alexandra Boulat), 41 bottom (P Macdiarmid), 46 (Sipa); Topham Picturepoint 3, 10, 12, 15 bottom, 17 (AP), 23 (Photri), 32, 33, 34, 36 (AP), 41 top (AP); TRH 39 (UN).

CONTENTS

ON AUGUST 1, 1990 THE SITUATION IN THE Persian Gulf region had reached a crisis point. For weeks, President Saddam Hussein, the ruler of the neighboring state of Iraq, had been making threats of invasion against the government of the tiny, oil-rich state of Kuwait. Oil was one of Saddam Hussein's main reasons for threatening Kuwait. Three-quarters of the world's oil reserves, which keep the wheels of the West's industries and cars turning, are to be found in the Middle East. Although Iraq had its own oil supplies, it still needed more cash and resources following the long, expensive war it had recently fought with the state of Iran.

Iraq's tanks roll down a road in Kuwait in the dawn light. Kuwait's lightly armed troops were able to offer only a token resistance to Iraq's vastly superior forces.

Other Arab rulers, such as President Mubarak of Egypt and King Hussein of Jordan, wanted to preserve peace in the Middle East. They tried to mediate, but failed. Iraq had massed 100,000 troops on Kuwait's frontier, but few people in the Middle East or elsewhere in the world believed it would really attack. The Charter of the Arab League, the international organization that includes all Arab states, forbids any Arab country to attack another.

Shortly after midnight on August 2, Saddam Hussein ordered his troops to cross Kuwait's border. Kuwait offered little resistance, and no help was forthcoming from its neighbors. Within a day, Iraq's hold on Kuwait was complete.

Shocked by this hostile action, international organizations and countries around the world immediately condemned Iraq. The United Nations Security Council called on it to withdraw. Then-president George Bush, said: "The United States strongly condemns the invasion and calls for an immediate withdrawal. There is no place for this kind of brutal aggression in today's world."

A Moment in Time

At 2 A.M. Kuwait time on August 2, 1990, Iraqi tanks enter Kuwait.

A Kuwaiti journalist watching from his balcony describes the scene: "When I looked out of my window I could see smoke billowing in the distance and could hear more machine-gun fire. We didn't realize what was going on until 6 A.M. when a statement was made by the Kuwaiti Defense Department. After that, there was mass panic, with people calling their relatives to see if everything was all right."

This map shows Iraq and its neighboring countries in the Middle East.

1000 miles

1000 km

Iraq's former president Saddam Hussein addresses his people in the Iraqi capital Baghdad. The Iraqi leader held power from 1979 to 2003. He was driven out by a U.S.-led invasion.

Saddam's Reasons for Invading Kuwait

- Saddam Hussein claimed that he had fought a war with Iran between 1980 and 1988 to provide protection against Iran for Kuwait and the other Gulf states, namely Bahrain, Qatar, the United Arab Emirates, Oman, and Saudi Arabia. He therefore wanted to be excused from paying his debts to Kuwait and the other Gulf states that had lent him money during the war.

- Iraq's debts were huge. Saddam claimed that Kuwait was forcing down oil prices by producing too much oil. The effect of this was to cut Iraq's income.

- Iraq needed better access to the Gulf. Saddam wanted to take possession of the two Kuwaiti islands of Bubiyan and Warbah, which faced the Iraqi port of Umm Qasr. Once in control of these, Saddam could build a deep-sea harbor to enable bigger ships to off-load cargos from Iraq and sail out freely into the Gulf.

- Saddam was aware of the claims of previous Iraqi governments, which had argued that, historically, the whole of Kuwait belonged to Iraq (see page 9).

Iraqi children play in front of a mural of Saddam Hussein in Baghdad on March 8, 1998. Before the Gulf War, Hussein accused the United States of wanting low-priced oil from Kuwait. He said: "We want stability and peace, but without pride, life would have no value."

Saddam Hussein (1937–)

Saddam Hussein was born on April 28, 1937 near Tikrit, 62 miles (100 kilometers) north of Baghdad. Although his village was poor—there was no electricity or running water—Saddam still received an education. In 1963 he became an official of the Baath Party. He spent a period of time in prison when the party was out of favor. When the Baath took power in 1968, Saddam was an important figure. He became president of Iraq on July 16, 1979, following the resignation of General Ahmed Hassan Al Bakr, one of his relatives. Following his rise to power, Saddam ordered the murder of all those in the government and the army who might be against him. Saddam was an adventurer, ready for any gamble he thought he might win. He was ambitious and ruthless, and a cruel dictator who behaved inhumanely to his enemies. He never hesitated to kill his opponents or anyone who dared to defy him.

UNTIL THE END OF WORLD WAR I (1914–1918), the territory that was eventually to become Iraq was made up of three Arab provinces: Mosul, Baghdad, and Basra. These provinces were ruled by Turkey as part of its Ottoman Empire. The Ottoman Empire had fought on the side of Germany during World War I, but had been defeated by the Allied Powers. British troops occupied the territory when the war ended in 1918.

In 1920 the League of Nations, the international body set up after World War I to help keep world peace, gave Great Britain the task of governing the former Ottoman provinces that made up the new country of Iraq. This was known as the League of Nations Mandate over Iraq. Britain's job was to control Iraq until the League of Nations believed that it was ready to become an independent country. In other words, Iraq needed to establish institutions and a government capable of the task of ruling. King Faisal I, an Arab leader who had helped Britain defeat Turkey, was crowned King of Iraq in 1921 in the capital city, Baghdad.

In 1932 Iraq became peacefully independent with Britain's agreement, though Britain maintained a strong influence over the country. But political change was to come to Iraq. In 1958 King Faisal II, the grandson of King Faisal I, was killed in a military coup and Iraq became a republic, a country without a monarch. In practice Iraq became a dictatorship under the rule of its president. In 1968 President Aref, Iraq's third military leader, was overthrown by the Iraqi branch of the Baath Party. This was an international and nonreligious Arab nationalist movement founded during World War II in Syria by a group of Muslim and Christian Arabs. General Ahmed Hassan Al Bakr, a Baathist former prime minister of Iraq and relative of Saddam Hussein, became president. Saddam Hussein rose to become Bakr's deputy, and took over as president in 1979. From 1980 to 1988, under Saddam's rule, Iraq was engaged in a war with its neighbor, the Islamic Republic of Iran.

Iraq is in many ways a modern country in which many people live in towns and enjoy a good standard of living working in offices and factories. Some of its people however, especially those in rural areas, live in poverty. Before 1990 Iraq had a bustling economy based on income from its oil industry, and had the beginnings of a flourishing industrial sector. Cars and televisions were common, and computer use was growing fast. Iraq's health service and education were the best in the Arab world. Almost all the people in the country were able to read and write. Since Iraq is a secular state, many

Iraqis wear Western dress and many women, especially in the towns, do not cover their hair or wear traditional Islamic clothing.

Successive Iraqi governments have argued that the tiny monarchy of Kuwait, which lies to the south of Iraq at the head of the Gulf, should be part of Iraq's territory. They have considered it historically to be part of the Iraqi province of Basra. In 1961 and 1973 Iraq made serious claims to be the rightful owner of Kuwait, and in 1973 British troops went to Kuwait to prevent a possible Iraqi invasion. If Iraq took over Kuwait, it would have much better access to the sea, enabling it to trade goods more freely, especially oil. As it stands, Iraq's principal port at Basra is 50 miles (80 kilometers) inland up the Shatt el-Arab waterway.

The main reason why Iraq wanted Kuwait, however, was oil. Of the world's total oil reserves, 25 percent are in Saudi Arabia, ten percent in Iraq, and ten percent in Kuwait. If Iraq had been able to take over Kuwait, it would control twenty percent of the world's oil—almost as much as Saudi Arabia.

Baghdad is a big city with a population of almost five million. Before 1990 it was a cosmopolitan capital, welcoming visitors from around the world.

KUWAIT, WITH ITS TWO MILLION INHABITANTS, IS Iraq's southern neighbor. It faces the waters of the Gulf and is mainly desert. It is hot, with temperatures soaring to 120°F (49°C) in the summer. Inland and to the south of Kuwait is Saudi Arabia, and across the Gulf lies Iran.

In 1899 Britain made a treaty with the ruler of Kuwait, at that time a trading port with a very loose connection to the Ottoman Empire. This treaty allowed the British government to make all major policy decisions for the Kuwaiti ruler. After World War I, Britain decided to maintain Iraq and Kuwait as separate states. Britain was in a position to do this because it controlled both sides of the frontier. This decision was the origin of Iraq's claim to Kuwait's territory. There was some force behind Iraq's argument because, although Kuwait had its own ruler, when it had been attached to the Ottoman Empire it had been part of the province of Basra.

For 250 years Kuwait has been ruled by the "Al Sabah," the Sabah family. However, after Britain's treaty with Kuwait in 1899, Britain effectively had control until 1961. Kuwait gained full independence from Britain on June 19, 1961, when the two countries agreed that the treaty between them should end. In a ceremony in Kuwait City, the new Kuwaiti flag was raised. When the link with Britain was broken, Kuwait was immediately threatened with annexation (takeover) by Iraq. British troops stayed until 1971 to defend the country.

In contrast with the republic of Iraq, Kuwait is ruled by a monarchy that doesn't want change. Islam is strictly observed. Kuwait is mainly Sunni Muslim, but some Shi'ite Muslims live there too. The wealth of Kuwait is evident in its modern buildings and American cars, contrasting with the traditional white robes worn by most men, usually with a *kefiyyeh*, a checkered headdress. The Islamic prohibition of alcohol is followed and many, but not all, women wear veils outdoors. Of Kuwait's inhabitants, 60 percent are foreigners, ranging from American oil workers and British accountants to Indian merchants and Bangladeshi workers.

Before the Iraqi invasion, life in Kuwait was luxurious for many of its people. Air conditioning and American cars were typical of the middle-class way of life. Since the end of the occupation in 1991, this standard of living has returned.

Women in Kuwait

There are conflicting images of women in Kuwait. Many dress in black veils and appear to be dependent on the men in their families. Although the Gulf is the most conservative part of the Muslim world, Kuwaiti women drive, are allowed to travel alone and to go abroad, and often work. Women hold jobs in administration, in business, and at academic institutions. Modern education has enhanced women's skills, and 41 percent of the graduates of Kuwait University are female. When Iraq occupied Kuwait, Kuwaiti women reacted immediately. The first women's demonstration protesting against the Iraqi presence came just two days after the occupation began, and other similar demonstrations followed. Kuwaiti women participated in the struggle against the Iraqi occupation alongside Kuwaiti men. After the liberation of the country, new challenges faced Kuwait and its people. From the time of Iraq's withdrawal, women have fought hard to gain the vote and political equality.

Kuwait's wealth comes from its oil industry, controlled by the state-owned Kuwait Petroleum Company. The ruling family and the country benefit from Kuwait's oil income.

Most Kuwaiti people live in Kuwait City, which originally was a fishing port and trading post. But the discovery of oil in 1938 changed everything. Since oil began to pour from Kuwait's wells, many people have become wealthy. The ruling Sabah family is immensely rich. But there are some poor Kuwaitis, including the bedouin (Arab tribesmen) and some residents without nationality, known as the *bidoon*, a word that means "without" in Arabic.

In the past, foreign companies ran Kuwait's oil wells. By the time Iraq invaded Kuwait in August 1990 the giant Kuwaiti company, KPC (Kuwait Petroleum Company), operated Kuwait's oil industry. At the same time, the KIO (Kuwait Investment Office) had become responsible for investing the state's money.

Kuwait has an elected parliament, or governing body, which advises the ruler on policy. However, the ruler appoints the government, and the prime minister is usually the Crown Prince, the ruler's heir. Parliament is elected by only a handful of Kuwait's citizens—those who can prove Kuwaiti ancestry before 1920. And, despite being promised the vote in the near future, women may neither vote nor sit in parliament.

Oil refining and storage installations in Kuwait. Many of these needed to be rebuilt after the departure of the Iraqi troops in 1991.

KUWAIT LIVES ON ITS INCOME FROM OIL. IRAQ on the other hand has oil, agriculture, and industry. In 1927 oil was discovered in northern Iraq. Over the years production expanded and, by the time of the events of 1990, Iraq had become one of the world's leading oil producers. Together with Saudi Arabia, Iraq and Kuwait were both founder members of OPEC, the Organization of Petroleum Exporting Countries, and of OAPEC, the Organization of Arab Petroleum Exporting Countries.

Three-quarters of the world's oil reserves are in the Middle East, mainly in the Gulf. Oil is vitally important to the world economy. The United States will increasingly depend on imported oil as its own supplies run out. As world oil reserves decrease, competition for the remaining oil supplies will increase and prices will rise. Oil is a natural resource that cannot be replaced, and there is concern that, later this century, supplies will not be sufficient to meet world needs.

Oil resources in the Middle East are divided among the Arab countries of the Gulf and Iran. The majority of the known reserves of oil in the Middle East, a quarter of the world's total, is held by Saudi Arabia, while Kuwait, Iraq, and Iran have nearly ten percent each. Smaller quantities of oil and gas are held by the United Arab Emirates, Qatar, and Oman. In comparison, the United States has less than four percent of the known reserves, while the countries of the former Soviet Union hold less than six percent. The rest of the world's oil is mainly concentrated in a few countries, including the African state of Nigeria, Venezuela in South America, and Malaysia in the Far East.

PRE-1990 OIL PRODUCTION IN BARRELS PER DAY (BPD)	
Kuwait	1.8 million bpd
Iraq	2.8 million bpd
Iran	2.9 million bpd
Saudi Arabia	5.1 million bpd
United States	8.5 million bpd

PRE-1990 OIL RESERVES	
Great Britain	0.4 percent
United States	3.4 percent
Iran	9.2 percent
Iraq	9.8 percent
Kuwait	9.9 percent
Saudi Arabia	25.2 percent

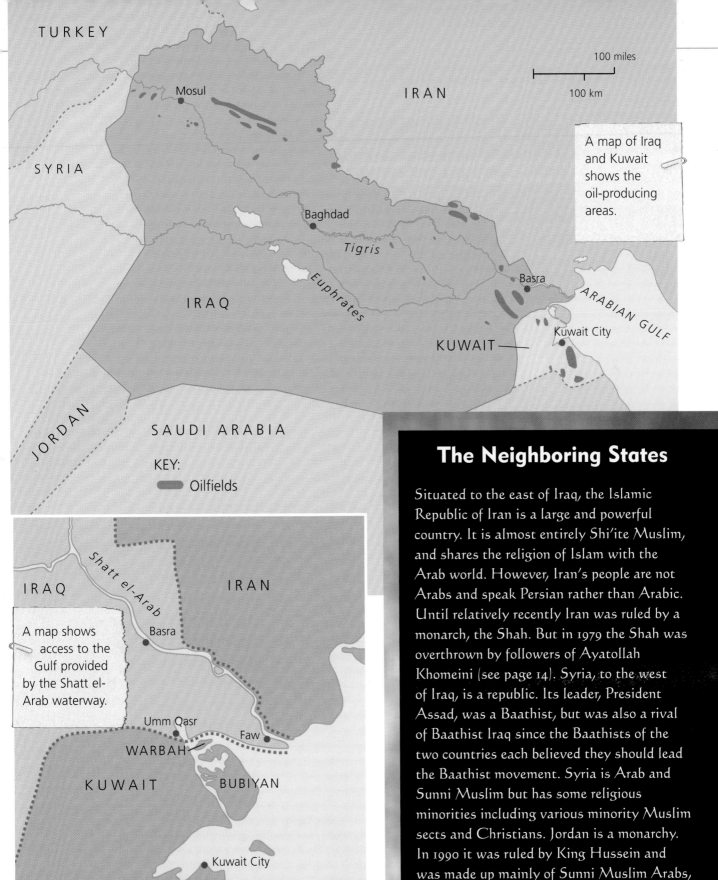

TURKEY

IRAN

Mosul

SYRIA

Baghdad

Tigris

Euphrates

IRAQ

Basra

ARABIAN GULF

KUWAIT

Kuwait City

JORDAN

SAUDI ARABIA

KEY:

Oilfields

100 miles

100 km

A map of Iraq
and Kuwait
shows the
oil-producing
areas.

IRAQ

Shatt el-Arab

IRAN

A map shows
access to the
Gulf provided
by the Shatt el-
Arab waterway.

Basra

Umm Qasr

Faw

WARBAH

KUWAIT

BUBIYAN

Kuwait City

ARABIAN GULF

50 miles

50 km

The Neighboring States

Situated to the east of Iraq, the Islamic
Republic of Iran is a large and powerful
country. It is almost entirely Shi'ite Muslim,
and shares the religion of Islam with the
Arab world. However, Iran's people are not
Arabs and speak Persian rather than Arabic.
Until relatively recently Iran was ruled by a
monarch, the Shah. But in 1979 the Shah was
overthrown by followers of Ayatollah
Khomeini (see page 14). Syria, to the west
of Iraq, is a republic. Its leader, President
Assad, was a Baathist, but was also a rival
of Baathist Iraq since the Baathists of the
two countries each believed they should lead
the Baathist movement. Syria is Arab and
Sunni Muslim but has some religious
minorities including various minority Muslim
sects and Christians. Jordan is a monarchy.
In 1990 it was ruled by King Hussein and
was made up mainly of Sunni Muslim Arabs,
together with Christian minorities. Turkey, to
the north, is almost entirely Sunni Muslim,
but the Turks are a separate people with a
language of their own. Turkey has its own
Kurdish minority.

Ayatollah Khomeini (standing in window with raised arm), Iran's religious leader, was Saddam Hussein's sworn enemy in the first Gulf War. The Islamic revolutionaries in Iran hated and despised the Baathist secular state in Iraq.

O N FEBRUARY 1, 1979, AYATOLLAH Khomeini returned to Tehran, the capital of Iran, from exile in Paris. Millions of people lined the road from Tehran's airport to the center of the city. Ayatollah Khomeini was a senior Shi'ite cleric (man of religion) who had been deported by the Shah, the former Iranian ruler. In the 1970s a revolution led by religious figures deposed the Shah, whose regime had become increasingly harsh and unpopular. Upon coming to power, Ayatollah Khomeini set up the Islamic Republic. Iranians claimed that this was the first state to be run entirely according to the principles of Islam. The new government in Iran said it intended to export the principles of its Islamic revolution to all Muslim states in the Middle East. Saddam Hussein saw this as a threat to his survival. The United States and some European countries also saw Islamic Iran as a threat to their interests and to stability in the region.

A Moment in Time

On the morning of February 1, 1979, the new leader of Iran, Ayatollah Khomeini, arrives in Tehran from exile in Paris. Chaotic scenes begin the moment his chartered Air France Boeing 747 aircraft lands. A group of welcoming clergy surrounds him, struggling to keep away all those they consider not fit to meet the new leader. Khomeini gives a speech that can scarcely be heard for the chanting of "Allahu Akbar" ("God is the most great"). The atmosphere is frenzied, and millions of people line the streets from the airport to Tehran. Khomeini's motorcade makes slow progress through frantic crowds hurling themselves against his car. When Khomeini reaches his headquarters near Tehran's parliament building, it is the dawning of a new era for Iran.

Iraqi war dead are taken for burial. The human costs of the eight-year Iran-Iraq war were enormous, with 375,000 Iraqi troops and at least 300,000 Iranians dead.

On September 22, 1980, Saddam launched a war on Iran. He believed Iran might invade Iraq or inspire an Islamic revolution inside Iraq against him. The Iranians quickly counterattacked. Although Saddam had hoped for a quick victory, the fighting lasted eight years with hundreds of thousands of dead on both sides. Iraq and Iran fired missiles at each other's capital cities and attacked each other's ships in the Gulf. Early in 1988 Saddam used chemical weapons against his own citizens, Iraqi Kurds at Halabja. He thought the Kurds might be helping Iran. Thousands of innocent civilians were killed in the attack.

In his war on Iran, Saddam Hussein was aided by most of the Arab states and by the West, which believed that any growth in Iran's power and influence could harm their interests. Although Iraq obtained money and assistance from Western countries, including the United States, there was a Western embargo (ban) on giving arms to Iraq. The war ended on August 16, 1988, when Iraq asked for a ceasefire.

From Iraq's point of view, the war had been a failure. Ayatollah Khomeini continued to rule, and the border between the two nations remained unchanged. Saddam Hussein still did not have sole possession of the disputed Shatt el-Arab waterway from Basra to the Gulf, though this had been one of his war goals.

Iranian prisoners of war return home. Many prisoners on both sides were held for years after their capture and were released long after the fighting ended.

During the war, Kuwait had given Iraq $12 billion in aid. But Iraq ended the war with debts of $80 billion, which it could not pay, including debts owed to Kuwait. Saddam Hussein thought that if he annexed Kuwait (joined it to his own territory) it would solve all his problems. It would enable him to pay his debts, provide him with a larger income, and he would seem to the Iraqi people to be a national hero. In this way, Iraq's war with Iran set the scene for Iraq's invasion of Kuwait.

Saddam Hussein visits a firing range with King Hussein of Jordan (kneeling). Once Saddam's closest friend in the Arab world, King Hussein tried to resolve the Gulf crisis peacefully. He was shunned for years by the West and the Gulf countries for refusing to abandon Saddam.

Between 1988 and 1990, after the end of the Iran-Iraq war, Saddam Hussein continued to be a source of concern to his Arab neighbors. Other Arab states regarded Iraq as difficult to deal with, and none doubted Saddam's brutality. Many people throughout the Arab world saw Saddam as a champion, but although most Arab governments still officially backed Saddam, they were fearful of him.

Some countries, however, were friendly with Iraq. King Hussein of Jordan had backed Iraq throughout the war with Iran. Jordan could not give money, like the rich Arab states of the Gulf, but it allowed Iraq to bring in supplies through Aqaba, Jordan's port on the Red Sea. Ali Abdullah Saleh, the ruler of Yemen, also admired Saddam. Egypt helped Iraq in the war, though more cautiously. In 1989 the states of Jordan, Yemen, and Egypt allied themselves with Iraq in a new regional grouping called the Arab Cooperation Council.

Hussein also continued to rely on the support of Western friends, such as the United States, Great Britain, and France, who had backed him during the Iran-Iraq war. The Western powers still believed that the biggest threat to their interests and to stability in the Middle East was from the Islamic Republic of Iran. Iraq was also a big market for Western exports, though arms-related goods were officially banned. The United States thought that Iraq would continue to protect the oil countries in the Gulf from Iran. Saddam also had support in cash and in arms supplies from the Soviet Union, which had backed him during the Cold War as a counter to U.S. influence in the Middle East. None of these countries realized that Iraq itself was a threat.

The Arab League

The Arab League, the international organization to which all Arab states belong, was set up in 1945 following World War II. Iraq was a founding member of the League, and Kuwait joined in 1961. The League promotes cooperation and unity among the Arab states and forbids the use of force to settle disputes between members. In the event of such a dispute, the Council of the Arab League has the power to decide what action to take. In practice, the Arab League tries not to reach conclusions unless all its members agree. As the crisis between Iraq and Kuwait developed in 1990, the Arab League became concerned that Iraq might be a threat to the stability of the Arab world. Saddam's habit of making threats worried the League, whose concerns were justified, as the invasion of Kuwait was later to show.

The Arab League in session in Cairo in March 1991. The invasion of Kuwait was not discussed at this meeting because the League did not want to see clashes between its members around the conference table.

Tariq Aziz was foreign minister of Iraq in 1991 and later became Iraq's deputy prime minister. He was a key spokesperson for Saddam Hussein and one of his closest advisers. Aziz came out of hiding and gave himself up to U.S. forces in April 2003, after the U.S.-led invasion of Iraq.

THE PRELUDE TO IRAQ'S INVASION OF KUWAIT stretched back over several months. No one can claim that the invasion could have been predicted but, looking at events with hindsight, the signs were there. At the Arab League summit in May 1990, Saddam Hussein had accused the other Arab oil-producing states of deliberately keeping the price of oil low in order to damage the Iraqi economy. Iraq's foreign minister, Tariq Aziz, a trusted friend of Saddam, had spoken out strongly at what he said was Arab treachery. He had bitterly criticized Kuwait for insisting on the settlement of Iraq's debts. Iraq began military exercises in the southern part of the country, but observers in the West and the Arab world thought this was just part of Iraq's threatening posture.

On July 24, 1990, Iraq began moving its troops toward the border with Kuwait. Still no one believed that Saddam planned to attack. On July 25 the United States ambassador, April Glaspie, met with Saddam. Her mission was to find out his intentions and communicate the U.S. position. Hindsight suggests that the United States did not sufficiently express its opposition to an invasion.

Saudi Arabia feared that trouble on its borders could endanger its own vast oil wealth. It made moves to persuade Iraq and Kuwait to negotiate. On July 31, talks took place between Saddam's deputy and Kuwait's Crown Prince at the Saudi Arabian port of Jeddah. These seemed to lead to some possibility of

Iraqi troops chant pro-Saddam and anti-American slogans as they get ready for war.

The former U.S. ambassador to Iraq, April Glaspie, was the last American diplomat to speak to Saddam Hussein before the invasion of Kuwait.

Dangerous Words

" I admire your extraordinary efforts to rebuild your country. I know you need funds. We understand that, and our opinion is that you should have the opportunity to rebuild your country. But we have no opinion on the Arab-Arab conflicts like your border disagreements with Kuwait. "

The words of U.S. Ambassador April Glaspie at her meeting with Saddam Hussein on July 25, 1990. Many believe that this meeting caused Saddam to believe that the United States would not interfere with his invasion of Kuwait.

compromise on the payment of Iraq's debts, but Kuwait refused to give up the two islands of Bubiyan and Warbah that Iraq had always claimed as its own. At the same time, other friends of Iraq were trying to resolve the clash between Iraq and Kuwait. King Hussein of Jordan and President Mubarak of Egypt met at the end of July, hoping to suggest a solution.

However, Saddam Hussein's mind was made up. He had been, some say, an adventurer all his life, and he was about to embark on his biggest escapade so far.

1:30 A.M. Kuwait time Iraqi tanks received the order to move. Within half an hour they had crushed the Kuwaiti frontier posts, crossed the border, and rolled on toward Kuwait City.

2:00 A.M. A British Airways flight bound for Malaysia with 367 passengers and 18 crew members on board touched down for a brief stopover at Kuwait International Airport, 9 miles (15 kilometers) south of the coastline, on the outskirts of Kuwait City. With Iraqi planes already overhead, commercial flights ceased. The British aircraft and its passengers would not be allowed to leave.

2:00 A.M. (7:00 P.M. Washington time) The news of the Iraqi invasion broke in Washington, D.C., on the evening of August 1, minutes after it had taken place. President Bush called an emergency meeting of his close security advisers for 11:30 P.M., and White House officials worked through the night. A problem was that Iraq had been regarded as a friend by the United States, and the Americans found it hard to decide how to respond to its hostile action. At 8:00 A.M. the next morning, Bush called a press conference and publicly condemned the invasion as "naked aggression."

2:30 A.M. Russia's foreign minister Edward Shevardnadze heard what had happened during the night as he flew from Irkutsk in Russia's far east to Moscow. At breakfast time in the Russian capital he called on Iraq to withdraw.

4:00 A.M. The ruler of Kuwait, Sheikh Jaber Al Ahmed Al Sabah, decided that resistance was impossible and began making his preparations to leave.

5:10 A.M. The Kuwaiti ruler escaped to Saudi Arabia by helicopter from the American embassy compound with the Crown Prince, Sheikh Saad. His younger brother, Sheikh Fahd, stayed behind and was killed in the fighting. Kuwait's ministry of defense, still functioning, asked Iraq to withdraw.

5:30 A.M. In the light of dawn, the Kuwaiti people were shocked and terrified as they saw the invaders in the streets. Kuwaiti radio continued to call for Arab assistance. The announcer's

In the early hours of August 2, 1990, the United Nations Security Council passes Resolution 660, condemning the Iraqi invasion.

On August 2 Iraq's forces take up their positions in Kuwait City, ready to crush any resistance.

voice was heard repeating: "The blood and honor of Kuwait has been violated: come to her aid!"

6:00 A.M. The Kuwaiti ministry of defense announced on Kuwaiti radio that the country had been invaded. The sound of gunfire could be heard across the city.

6:00 A.M. The airport was occupied by Iraqi troops and closed. The British Airways flight for Malaysia stood trapped on the runway. The passengers and crew were later taken to Iraq and used as hostages, though all hostages were freed by the end of December.

6:00 A.M. At 11:00 P.M. New York time, delegates to the United Nations (UN) were summoned to a late-night session at the UN's Manhattan headquarters. At 4:00 A.M. New York time on August 2, nine hours after the invasion had begun, the UN Security Council passed Resolution 660, condemning the actions of Iraq. Fourteen of the fifteen member states of the UN Security Council voted for the resolution, with only Yemen abstaining. The resolution called on Iraq to withdraw its troops and begin immediate talks with Kuwait on resolving the differences between the two states.

7:00 A.M. The Iraqi government announced on Baghdad radio that there was a revolution in Kuwait and claimed that Iraq's troops had entered Kuwait at the request of a new government. No evidence ever supported this claim. In the Iraqi capital, Baghdad, people awoke to hear the news of the invasion. They were overjoyed. After the failure in Iran two years before, the public was ready for an Iraqi success. Drivers honked their horns and flashed their lights in celebration as they drove to work.

7:00 A.M. Four loud explosions were heard in Kuwait City, followed by the sound of gunfire.

8:00 A.M. Some Kuwaitis, stunned by the news of the invasion or unaware that it had happened, tried to go to work as usual, but the Iraqi troops turned them back. Some found themselves facing Iraqi tanks and had to abandon their cars at gunpoint.

9:00 A.M. Many people went out into the streets, but normal life had come to a halt. Offices and workplaces were closed. Stores opened up, and people bought large amounts of food at the supermarkets. Some Kuwaitis tried to drive out of the country and into Saudi Arabia, but were turned back.

10:00 A.M. Iraqi troops were by now surrounding government offices, including the National Assembly (Kuwait's parliament), the Ministry of Defense, and the Ministry of Information, as well as other key points in the city. The British and American embassies were also surrounded by Iraqi troops. The National Bank was looted. Helicopters hovered low over the streets.

10:30 A.M. The Kuwaiti national guard made its last stand at the Dasman Palace, the official residence of the ruler of Kuwait, Sheikh Jaber, and a symbolic objective important for the Iraqis to capture. Fierce fighting took place and black smoke billowed from the building. By the end of the day, the palace was wrecked and looted.

11:00 A.M. The skies by now were dominated by Iraqi jets, flying freely over the whole country.

2:00 P.M. By this time, the streets were once again deserted. Offices and workshops were closed and store owners

Claims of Revolution

By noon on August 2, Iraq had begun to claim that there had been a popular revolution in Kuwait in favor of Iraq. It had named a Kuwaiti provisional government, but no citizens of Kuwait had agreed to take part in it. Some of the names announced for the ministers were actually Iraqis, and others were Kuwaiti bedouins, who did not hold full citizenship, or bidoon, who have no nationality. Iraq's information minister Latif Jasim said: "The world should forget a place called the Emirate of Kuwait." In an announcement from Kuwait radio, now in Iraqi hands, a spokesman said the ruler of Kuwait had been deposed and the former national assembly dissolved. The pretense that there was a new government in Kuwait was soon abandoned, and less than a week later Saddam Hussein announced that Kuwait had been annexed to Iraq.

Kuwait's ruler, Sheikh Jaber Al Ahmed Al Sabah fled from Kuwait during the invasion and returned on March 14, 1991.

The USS *Independence*: America's naval might was soon brought into play against Iraq in the Gulf.

were pulling down their steel shutters. Residents reported that some shops were looted. The telephones still worked, and since the morning Kuwaitis had been calling each other to exchange scraps of news and to check on friends and family. Most were very afraid. A secret Kuwaiti radio station was still broadcasting and would do so until the following day.

3:00 P.M. Many more Iraqi troops had now arrived, transported from the border in buses down roads controlled by Iraqi forces. Roadblocks stopped the traffic from moving, except for Iraqi military vehicles. Some Iraqis raced through the streets in jeeps, cheering and waving Iraqi flags.

7:30 P.M. By nightfall there was no question that the Iraqis were in total control. Citizens were banned from leaving their houses after dark. Gunfire could still be heard in the city during the night, especially from the eastern district where there were Kuwaiti army camps.

Meanwhile, around the world, reaction was beginning to accelerate.

During the morning of August 2, the U.S. aircraft carrier *Independence* began to sail toward the Gulf from the Indian Ocean, with its battle group of smaller ships. The U.S. government banned all imports into the United States from Iraq, including oil. It also froze Iraqi assets, which involved refusing to allow

any Iraqi-owned businesses or bank accounts in the United States to operate. Britain called on Iraq to withdraw its troops, threatening that the international community would take further action. The Soviet news agency, TASS, announced a halt of Russian arms exports to Iraq. France announced that it would put a freeze on all Iraqi assets.

Lebanon was the first Arab state to call on Iraq to withdraw. Hamid Al Ghabid, the secretary-general of the Organization of the Islamic Conference, a world body to which all countries with majority Muslim populations belong, called on Iraq to end its invasion. King Hussein of Jordan went to Egypt for talks with President Mubarak to promote what he called an Arab solution to the crisis. He hoped that the West would hold back, giving him time to persuade Saddam Hussein to pull out. Syria asked for an Arab League summit.

The foreign ministers of the Arab League met in the Egyptian capital Cairo, with senior Iraqi officials present. Iraq's deputy prime minister, Saadoun Hammadi, said the meeting was directed against Iraq's interests. As the day wore on, other Arab states issued their separate condemnations of Iraq. Finally, on the evening of August 2, Kuwait's Crown Prince, Sheikh Saad Al Abdullah Al Sabah, broadcast from Saudi Arabia that Kuwait would fight on. However, Saudi Arabia had not yet spoken out against Iraq.

As dawn broke on Friday August 3, ordinary Kuwaitis didn't know what to do. Though there had long been rumblings of trouble on the border with Iraq, no one had really believed that Saddam Hussein would launch an attack. Some say that the invasion also came as a surprise to most Iraqis, and that up until the order to attack came, most of the Iraqi troops believed they were on a military exercise. The Iraqi military command ordered Kuwaiti officials to continue their work under Iraqi orders. Individual Kuwaitis either bravely demonstrated against their occupiers or carried out small attacks against the Iraqi troops. Resistance fighters were killed if they were caught. The Iraqis also detained individuals they regarded as dangerous. The Iraqi soldiers on occasion behaved with brutality toward the civilians, but many of the more extreme stories later proved to be untrue.

On August 4 Saudi troops were put on the highest state of alert, as it was rumored that Iraq intended to press its invasion into Saudi Arabia. Twenty thousand Iraqi troops were stationed at the Saudi border with Kuwait. The United States warned Iraq not to attack Saudi Arabia, and for the first time explicitly threatened military action. The following day, President Bush once more demanded an immediate Iraqi withdrawal. The U.S. administration was now pressing Saudi Arabia to join in action against Iraq.

Saudi Arabia was highly cautious, but agreed to cooperate with the Americans.

On August 6 the United Nations Security Council passed Resolution 661, imposing sanctions on Iraq. The only state that did not vote for the resolution was Iraq's friend Yemen. On August 7 President Bush received the Saudi leadership's permission to station U.S. and allied troops in Saudi Arabia and ordered the first U.S. troops to the Gulf.

George Bush (1924–)

George Bush (father of President George W. Bush) was elected president of the United States in 1988 and took office in January 1989. Bush had served as vice-president in President Ronald Reagan's Republican administration. He was a former diplomat and, in the 1970s, was director of the CIA (Central Intelligence Agency). In 1990 he knew many of the Middle East leaders personally. He presided over the difficult period of relations with the former Soviet Union as it broke into separate states after 1989. His major achievement following the Gulf War was to convene the Madrid conference in 1991. This began the Middle East peace process, which tried to reconcile Israel and the Palestinians.

Property and buildings in Kuwait were extensively damaged in the Iraqi attack. Kuwait is still demanding full compensation.

On August 23 1990 Saddam Hussein spoke on Iraqi TV to one of his hostages, five-year-old Stuart Lockwood, a British boy taken prisoner along with his mother when a British passenger plane was seized in Kuwait.

The first U.S. troops began to arrive in Saudi Arabia on August 8. Arab and European troops would soon follow. President Bush addressed the American people on television, announcing that he planned to take action against Iraq. He used the memorable phrase: "A line has been drawn in the sand." Meanwhile the Iraqi government abandoned the pretense that there had been a popular uprising in Kuwait, and issued a proclamation stating that Kuwait was now part of Iraq. The Palestinian leader Yasser Arafat flew to Baghdad, where he pledged his support but advised Saddam to try to avoid war.

On August 10 the UN Security Council's Resolution 662 unanimously condemned Iraq's unilateral annexation of Kuwait. In Cairo, the Arab League summit meeting demanded by most Arab states was held. The meeting refused to recognize Iraq's annexation of Kuwait. Saddam made a defiant speech on Iraqi television, attacking the United States, and for the first time declaring that his action in Kuwait was a "Holy War" on behalf of all Muslims. He ordered all foreign embassies in Kuwait to close, and all diplomats to leave by August 24.

King Hussein of Jordan spoke on Jordanian television to condemn the arrival of U.S. troops in Saudi Arabia. He said that the Arabs should be left to resolve their own problems and alleged that the United States was interested only in protecting its oil supplies. As the days passed, only Jordan, Yemen, and the Palestine Liberation Organization continued to offer any support to Iraq.

Iraq announced that it would be the "host" of all foreign citizens who had been in Iraq or Kuwait at the time of the crisis. In other words, the foreigners would be used as a "human shield" against attack. However, Saddam freed the women and children in September, and the men during December when he realized his ploy would not save him from attack.

On August 25 the UN Security Council passed Resolution 665, authorizing the use of force to halt shipping trading with Iraq. Three days later, Iraq's parliament announced that it had passed legislation declaring Kuwait to be the nineteenth province of Iraq. Kuwait would now be part of the Iraqi state in the same way as the other eighteen provinces.

ON SEPTEMBER 9 A MEETING TOOK PLACE IN THE Finnish capital, Helsinki, between President Bush and President Gorbachev of the Soviet Union. The Soviet leader gave his backing to the U.S. plan to remove Iraq from Kuwait, by diplomacy or by force. This was the first time the leaders of the world's two superpowers had made such an agreement at a time of international crisis. President Bush agreed that President Gorbachev would stay in direct contact with Iraq, using the Soviet Union's existing relations with Iraq to keep a channel of communication open.

A few days later, the British government announced that it was sending 6,000 British troops and 120 tanks to the Gulf to join the U.S. forces. France revealed that it was sending more ships to the Gulf and would send 3 regiments, 100 antitank helicopters and 14 ships, bringing its forces, including its fleet, to a total of 13,000 troops. Egypt increased its contribution to the alliance to 20,000 troops, and Syria also agreed to send a small contingent of soldiers.

In a speech on Iraqi television on September 23, Saddam Hussein threatened to destroy Kuwait's oilfields if his army was forced to leave. He also linked the situation in Kuwait with the issue of peace between Israel and the Arabs. He would leave Kuwait, he said, if Israel would withdraw from all the Palestinian territory it had occupied in 1967. In an address to the United Nations, the ruler of Kuwait, Sheikh Jaber, compared the Iraqi invasion with Israel's occupation of the West Bank since 1967 and its invasion of southern Lebanon in 1982.

At the UN headquarters in New York, French President Mitterand suggested a plan to discuss all aspects of the crisis in the Middle East, including the issue of peace between the Israelis and the Palestinians, after an Iraqi withdrawal from Kuwait. Meanwhile the price of oil, which had been steadily rising, briefly hit a record level of $40 per barrel. Before the crisis broke out, the price was around $21 per barrel.

On October 16 President Bush warned Saddam Hussein that he could be held responsible for war crimes committed in Kuwait. This warning was followed on October 20 by a visit to Baghdad by the former British prime minister Edward Heath, who asked Saddam Hussein to release the European and American men still held hostage by Iraq.

On November 22 President Bush visited U.S. troops in Saudi Arabia for Thanksgiving. After inspecting the U.S. command headquarters in Dahran, an American

President George Bush in Saudi Arabia with U.S. soldiers on November 22, 1990. The president ate his Thanksgiving dinner with the troops and visited front-line units.

base in the desert, and a warship in the Gulf, he ate his Thanksgiving dinner with a group of American and British troops. The president said the American and allied troops would stay at their posts until their objective, the expulsion of Iraqi troops from Kuwait, had been reached. On November 29 the UN Security Council passed Resolution 678. This authorized the use of force against Iraq. It also gave Iraq a deadline, January 15, 1991, by which time all its troops were expected to have left Kuwait.

President Bush proposed that there should be direct talks between the United States and Iraq. He invited the Iraqi foreign minister, Tariq Aziz, to come to Washington, D.C. on December 10, and suggested that the U.S. secretary of state, James Baker, should visit Baghdad. But it was not until January 1991 that direct talks between the two sides took place.

Thoughts of the Soldiers

On August 28, 1990, U.S. troops arriving in Saudi Arabia say how they feel about their assignment:

" We're just here to do our job, again. It's the same ... thing, one guy causing all the trouble. "

" I've got a three-year-old girl at home and it was hard leaving her, but we joined the army to serve our country. "

" I'm going to miss my boyfriend and my family. I've been crying all the way here. "

" Me, I'm a single guy. I get paid good for what I do. It's a job and an adventure. "

American troops flew into Saudi Arabia in successive waves, from August to November, to begin training for desert warfare alongside their Saudi and British allies.

American Secretary of State James Baker (far right of photo) faces Iraqi Foreign Minister Tariq Aziz (center left) across the table in Geneva, Switzerland, on January 9, 1991.

Javier Perez de Cuellar (1920–)

Javier Perez de Cuellar, a Peruvian diplomat, was selected as UN secretary general in 1982. He was born in 1920 and went to college at a young age, becoming a diplomat in 1940. He then rose to be director of political affairs in the Peruvian foreign ministry. He helped to resolve the war between Iraq and Iran, but had less success with the Gulf War. While the crisis was underway, he negotiated with Saddam Hussein but failed to secure Iraq's withdrawal from Kuwait. He left his post in 1992 and went into politics in Peru.

THE UN SECRETARY GENERAL, JAVIER PEREZ de Cuellar of Peru, welcomed President Bush's proposal for direct talks with Iraq. From Rome, Pope John Paul II called for the opening of a dialogue. In December the foreign ministers of Egypt, Saudi Arabia, and Syria met in Cairo to discuss the Arab commitment to the alliance. The leaders of the European Union countries, meeting in Rome, issued a statement backing the United Nations resolutions that called for complete Iraqi withdrawal from Kuwait. U.S. Secretary of State James Baker said that only this would resolve the crisis.

King Hussein of Jordan issued a statement calling for an Arab dialogue to be held. He also called for talks between the United States and Iraq, and for an international conference on the Arab-Israeli dispute to be held as Iraqi forces withdrew from Kuwait. However, by January 1991 it had become increasingly clear that the crisis was unlikely now to be concluded in any way other than through war. Nevertheless, diplomacy went on. Face-to-face talks between James Baker and Iraq's

Tariq Aziz were held in neutral Switzerland. These were the only direct talks between the United States and Iraq during the course of the crisis. The two sides talked for six hours, but reached no agreement.

On January 13, Perez de Cuellar saw Saddam Hussein in Baghdad in a last-ditch attempt to find a peaceful solution to the crisis. Again, no breakthrough was reached. On January 16, the deadline set by the UN for Iraq's withdrawal from Kuwait expired. The scene was set for the beginning of war. The next day Saddam said in a speech on radio and television in Iraq that what he called "the mother of all battles" had now begun.

The Military Build-Up

From the moment the decision was made to drive the Iraqis out by force, the United States put aside its diplomatic efforts and amassed a huge military presence. By the end of September 1990, there were 300,000 Iraqi troops in Kuwait. The U.S. troop buildup soon reached a similar figure. By the end of October 1990, there were 275,000 allied troops, including 200,000 Americans. The main allies were Saudi Arabia, Britain, and France. Arab forces came from Egypt, Morocco, Syria, and other countries that had voted for the Arab League resolution to intervene. Those Kuwaiti soldiers who had been able to flee the country also joined. By November, the allied forces totaled 500,000. The United States used civilian aircraft and military transport planes to move troops in faster. Iraq responded by increasing its forces in Kuwait to 430,000, though before the land war began in February 1991, Iraq pulled out many of its elite troops. The American-led allies totaled 534,000, including 205,000 non-American troops from 39 countries.

British troops in desert training in Saudi Arabia, where they were a significant part of the coalition forces.

THE UNITED NATIONS HAD SET A FINAL DEADLINE, January 15, 1991, for Saddam Hussein to withdraw his troops from Iraq. Saddam chose to ignore it. Instead, on January 14 the Iraqi parliament met to give its backing to Saddam's policies. On the evening of January 16, Washington time, President Bush launched the alliance's air attack on Iraq and on the occupying forces in Kuwait. The operation known as "Desert Storm" had begun.

In the early hours of January 17, allied ships in the Gulf launched their cruise missiles, and at about 2:30 A.M. Iraq time, antiaircraft guns were heard in Baghdad. United States and British aircraft were striking at military targets all over Iraq. In response, Iraq launched Scud missile attacks against Israel and Saudi Arabia.

Despite the dangers, some Western journalists still remained in the Iraqi capital. On the first day of the conflict, reports from Baghdad were broadcast live on Cable News Network (CNN).

The Outbreak of War

" I looked outside the hotel window and saw silvery pieces floating from the sky; instantly I knew it was radar-jamming chaff, designed to prevent radar from detecting planes. Then antiaircraft batteries surrounding the hotel began firing frantically and aimlessly into the black sky. Air-raid sirens wailed and I became very angry because I knew I had no control over my safety or fate and I knew the war was now underway. "

In an interview on January 16, 2001, American journalist Bernard Shaw remembers the first moments of the war. Shaw was in Baghdad to interview Saddam Hussein for CNN. He was able to broadcast from his hotel room at the Al Rasheed Hotel until Iraq cut the links. He was one of three journalists who provided continuous live coverage of the allied bombing for several hours until Iraqi security cut communications.

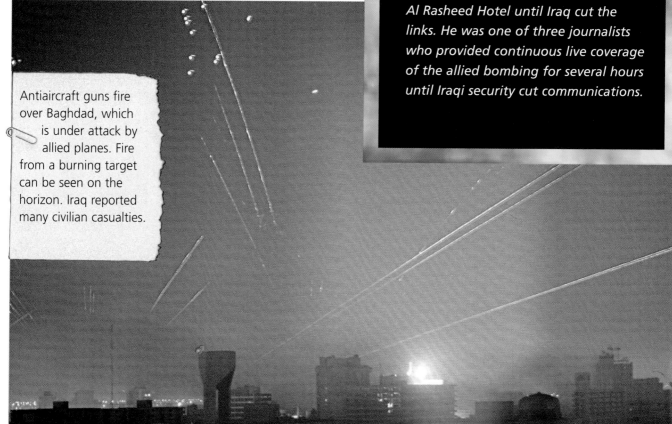

Antiaircraft guns fire over Baghdad, which is under attack by allied planes. Fire from a burning target can be seen on the horizon. Iraq reported many civilian casualties.

Iraqi soldiers dug in at the front, waiting for the allied attack. Iraq's defensive line was swept away with no real resistance .

The aerial pounding of Iraq was to continue for more than a month. So-called "smart" bombs hit their targets with great accuracy. Unfortunately other attacks were less accurate, and there were civilian casualties. On January 30 Saddam Hussein reminded the United States that when the armies clashed on the ground there would be what he called "the mother of all battles."

On February 24 the ground attack began and allied troops moved to reoccupy Kuwait City. There was little resistance. Iraqi troops held out at the airport for two days. Saddam Hussein had withdrawn his best troops, the Republican Guard, and left mainly conscripts to fight. Iraqi forces surrendered in large numbers.

On February 26 U.S. and Saudi troops began to pursue the fleeing Iraqis northward. As the Iraqis retreated, many were killed on the road to Basra. On February 27 the allied commander General Norman Schwarzkopf said allied casualties had been "miraculously light." On February 28 President Bush ordered a ceasefire. The war was at an end. Kuwait was liberated, the royal family returned, and the Kuwaiti government was reestablished.

The aftermath of what allied troops called the "turkey shoot" north of Mutla Ridge, on the road to Basra. On February 26, 1991, Iraqi troops were attempting to flee northward in whatever vehicles they could find when they were caught by a fierce allied attack.

On March 14, 1991 the ruler of Kuwait, Sheikh Jaber Al Ahmed Al Sabah, went back to his country. Life in Kuwait began to return to normal. But there were serious problems. Before they left, Iraqi troops had set fire to the oil wells. There was damage to 732 wells, and spectacular flames burned day and night, filling the sky with black smoke. Huge quantities of oil flooded out into the desert. The Iraqis had also released oil into the Gulf. The aim was to do as much damage as possible to Kuwait's oil industry, in what was called a "scorched earth" policy.

Oil production in Kuwait temporarily closed down, and it was later estimated that the loss in revenue to Kuwait was $125 million a day. It took the Kuwaitis until the end of 1992 to get oil production back to normal. They were assisted by a team led by American expert Red Adair, who stopped each fire in turn with a controlled explosion.

The pollution from the oil fires affected people's health in Kuwait, and effects were observed as far away as Afghanistan. The oil leaks also harmed wildlife and seemed to cause short-term damage to fish stocks in the Gulf. The scientific evidence about pollution shows that there was massive damage to the fragile desert habitat. The movement of tanks and military vehicles destroyed the desert surface and landmines became a lasting problem. Hidden from view below the sand, the mines are difficult to find and continued to cause civilian casualties. The immediate effects of spilled and burning oil were catastrophic and soil, vegetation, wildlife, and water supplies all suffered. Fortunately, long-term damage has not been as severe as some predicted, though

Blazing oil wells are left by the retreating Iraqi army, who attempted to destroy Kuwait's oil production before leaving.

Saudi Arabia had to invest $450 million to clean up its coastline near Kuwait.

On the international markets, oil prices at first rose because of fears around the world that oil supplies might run short. Concerns that this might happen again were soon resolved when the OPEC countries raised their production to fill the gap caused by the temporary inactivity of Iraq and Kuwait. By June 1991, the price of a barrel of oil had fallen to $20, roughly what it had been before the war.

In the longer term, the Gulf War has had little effect on the oil market. Kuwait returned to full production in 1993, and since 1995 Iraq has been allowed to export a limited amount of oil, under United Nations supervision, to raise revenue to pay for essential food and medicine.

Average Monthly Oil Prices, 1990–1991

May	$16 per barrel
June	$17 per barrel
July	$19 per barrel
August	$26 per barrel
September	$36 per barrel
October	$37 per barrel
November	$36 per barrel
December	$30 per barrel
January	$22 per barrel
February	$20 per barrel
March	$19 per barrel
April	$20 per barrel
May	$18 per barrel

Oil released into the Gulf damaged the marine environment, while the smoke from burning oil wells polluted the skies.

British and American fighter aircraft patrol the no-fly zones set up after the war to curb Iraqi military activity and protect Iraq's Kurdish and Shi'ite communities.

THE ALLIES DID NOT PURSUE the Iraqi forces further toward Baghdad for a number of reasons. President Bush wanted the fighting to stop because he did not want to kill more Iraqi conscript soldiers. Furthermore, the goal of Desert Storm, to end the Iraqi occupation of Kuwait, had been achieved. President Bush did not want to be accused of invading Iraq.

On March 3, 1991, the ceasefire was confirmed when the Iraqi military commanders met with General Schwarzkopf at Safwan in southern Iraq. On April 3 the UN Security Council passed Resolution 687, which laid down the rules for Iraq that have applied ever since. Resolution 687 instructed Iraq to destroy its weapons of mass destruction and long-range missiles, and called on it to respect its international frontier with Kuwait and to pay Kuwait compensation for damage caused by the war. Until these conditions were fulfilled, the resolution banned Iraq from

trading, except for food imports. This is what is meant by the United Nation "sanctions" on Iraq. The UN has never been satisfied that Iraq has obeyed the resolution and the ban on trade with Iraq remained in place. However, since December 1996 Iraq has been allowed to export a limited amount of oil to enable it to buy food and medicines.

Since the invasion of Kuwait had made it clear that Saddam Hussein was a threat to peace in the Middle East, why was he left in place as leader of Iraq? At the time, the United States did not believe an invasion of Iraq would be the right way to change the regime in Baghdad. As General de la Billière, the commander of the British forces pointed out, there was a danger that: "Desert Storm could have been seen purely as an operation to further Western interests in the Middle East." Also, if Saddam were removed, who would replace him? There was an Iraqi opposition in exile, but U.S. policymakers did not believe that it would be able to run the country.

Nevertheless the United States did take some steps to protect Iraq's vulnerable people from Saddam. Following Iraq's defeat, the Kurdish people in the mountainous north of the country rose up against Saddam in March 1991. The United States sent in a force to give them some protection, and the Kurds were encouraged to set up their own government. Meanwhile in the south of the country, the southern Shi'ite peoples were less fortunate. They also rose in revolt against Saddam in March 1991 but their rebellion was crushed by Iraqi troops, without any intervention on the part of the allies.

The following year, so-called "no-fly zones" were set up by the United States. These covered the north and south of Iraq, where Iraqi aircraft were forbidden to go. The goal was to limit Iraq's ability to attack the Kurds and the Shi'ites. The Kurds enjoyed some security in northern Iraq, but the Shi'ites were not protected successfully by the southern no-fly zone and were effectively ruled by Saddam Hussein for many years. In addition, the wetlands where Iraq's unique population of Marsh Arabs lived have been drained. However, U.S. and British aircraft continued to patrol these zones and sometimes attacked Iraqi ground targets such as radar sites.

The Kurds

The Kurdish people live mainly in northern Iraq and southeastern Turkey. A few live in Syria and Iran. After World War I, the victorious Allied Powers (led by Britain, France, and the United States) divided up the Kurdish lands among other countries. The Kurds have therefore been struggling to achieve their independence for the past 80 years. They have two main political organizations, the Kurdish Democratic Party and the Patriotic Union of Kurdistan. Each of these governs part of the Kurdish territory in northern Iraq.

A Kurdish guerrilla gunner fires his field gun at an enemy position.

Iraq's principal Arab ally was Jordan. As early as August 3, King Hussein of Jordan had pleaded with President Bush for 48 hours to try to find what he called an "Arab solution" to the crisis. King Hussein went at once to Baghdad to speak with Saddam Hussein, but failed to persuade him to withdraw.

Jordan's support sprang from its historic ties with Iraq. King Hussein was to say frequently during the tense months following the invasion: "Our two countries are as one family." There was another reason why King Hussein was against the war. Half of Jordan's population was made up of Palestinians. They were especially anti-American because of the United States' support for Israel, and therefore opposed the war. On August 11, 1990, an American television correspondent reported from a Palestinian refugee camp that: "Saddam Hussein is winning over the masses."

Jordan suffered for its stand against the United States. It lost its financial support from the Gulf countries and was flooded with Palestinian refugees from Kuwait, Saudi Arabia, and the other Gulf countries. Palestinians occupied many professional and managerial posts in these countries, but were suddenly regarded as traitors because the Palestinian leadership supported Iraq.

Across the Arab world, although many governments backed the American-led alliance against Iraq, a large number of ordinary people did not approve of it. This was certainly the case in Egypt, Morocco, and Syria, where the governments had opted to support the United States.

The war also had its effect on the ongoing Middle East problem of hostility between Israel and its Arab neighbors. Israel was drawn into the conflict early in 1991. From January 18 onward, the Iraqis began

Palestine Liberation Organization chairman Yasser Arafat

A Moment in Time

On August 2, 1990 Yasser Arafat, the chairman of the Palestine Liberation Organization, receives a phone call at his home in Tunis from Palestinians living in Kuwait. They report details of an Iraqi invasion. Then the phone lines out of Kuwait go dead. Arafat decides to give his support to Iraq and sets off at once to visit Iraq and other Arab states. As far as his own people are concerned, Arafat's political judgment proves to be sound. In the occupied territories, Palestinians dance for joy when they hear the news of the invasion. But Arafat's apparent support for Iraq will cost him the goodwill and financial support he previously received from the Gulf countries.

firing long-range Scud missiles at Israeli targets. In all, Iraq fired 43 Scuds at Israel, targeting Tel Aviv and other cities. (In addition, 40 Scuds were fired at targets in Saudi Arabia.) But the United States urged Israel not to take any military part in the conflict, because the United States needed to keep the loyalty of its Arab allies.

The war did benefit the Palestinians and the Arab states in one way. In order to get the Arabs on his side, President Bush promised to reopen the question of Middle East peace and hold a conference. This was convened in Madrid in October 1991.

King Hussein of Jordan (1935–1999)

King Hussein was crowned in 1953 at the age of eighteen. He was the grandson of Jordan's founder, King Abdullah I. Britain had close relations with Jordan and helped King Hussein to keep his throne during difficult times in the 1950s. King Hussein was also very close to the United States. He held frequent meetings with all of the U.S. presidents from President Eisenhower onward, and received substantial U.S. military and economic aid. He owned houses in London and Washington, D.C., and was very much at home in the West. He died of cancer in February 1999 after returning to Jordan following a period of hospital treatment in the United States.

Many Israelis wore gas masks during the fighting, fearing that Saddam Hussein would launch missiles equipped with chemical warheads against Israel.

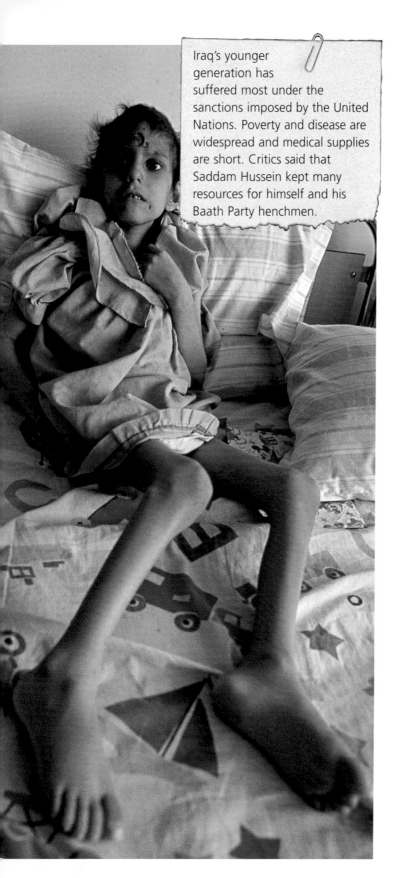

Iraq's younger generation has suffered most under the sanctions imposed by the United Nations. Poverty and disease are widespread and medical supplies are short. Critics said that Saddam Hussein kept many resources for himself and his Baath Party henchmen.

SINCE THE END OF THE GULF WAR, RELATIONS between the West and Iraq have been tense. In theory, Iraq accepted UN Resolution 687, requiring the removal of all weapons of mass destruction from its territory. But Saddam Hussein remained aggressive and hostile, avoiding full compliance with the resolution, and it appeared that he was no less brutal to his own people.

At the same time, the United Nations sanctions and the ban on trade reduced Iraq to poverty. Though Iraq had limited oil income, ordinary Iraqis were short on many things. Even with food rationing in place, children suffered particularly. Child mortality increased sharply.

On January 10, 1998, Pope John Paul II condemned the enforcement of United Nations sanctions. He spoke of "our brothers and sisters in Iraq, living under a pitiless embargo ... The weak and the innocent cannot pay for mistakes for which they are not responsible." Some UN officials agreed that the effect of the sanctions was too harsh. Dennis Halliday, the former United Nations humanitarian coordinator in Iraq, resigned his post in September 1998 because of this.

Meanwhile Saddam and his cronies lived in great luxury. The only prosperous Iraqis were officials of the ruling Baath Party and a handful of privileged businessmen. Iraq spent the money it had on maintaining and improving its military forces.

The condition for lifting the sanctions on Iraq was that it had to show that it had followed UN resolutions. These resolutions demanded the disposal of Iraq's weapons of mass destruction and their means of delivery. Iraq played cat-and-mouse games with the teams of UN-appointed inspectors who were sent to make sure weapons were being destroyed. On August 5, 1998, Iraq announced that it would no longer cooperate with the arms inspectors, who then left the country, to return only in November 2002.

The poverty of ordinary Iraqis aroused sympathy around the world. But many Arab states believed that the advantages gained by removing Saddam Hussein from power would be outweighed by the chaos that would follow if he left. Saddam therefore hoped he might get the sanctions lifted by political persuasion. But Saddam faced the determination of the United States to keep up the pressure on him to disarm or step down. Throughout the 1990s, the United States continued to say it wanted a change of leadership in Iraq. However, if anything, Saddam strengthened his grip on power. Saddam's position in 2003 looked increasingly insecure. President George W. Bush (son of the President Bush who had presided over the Gulf War) made it clear that he was determined to disarm Iraq and remove Saddam Hussein by force if necessary, whether the United Nations agreed or not.

The Weapons Issue

" Iraq must accept the destruction or removal of all chemical and biological weapons, and nuclear material .... The embargo on food is removed. Other sanctions will be lifted after weapons are removed. An arms embargo is maintained. "

From Resolution 687, agreed to by the United Nations Security Council on April 3, 1991

" The Security Council decides to afford Iraq a final opportunity to comply with its disarmament obligations ... and accordingly decides to set up an enhanced inspection regime with the aim of bringing to ... completion the disarmament process established by Resolution 687. "

From Resolution 1441, agreed to on November 8, 2002

UN weapons inspectors dispose of chemical weapons in Iraq. These warheads may have been designed to contain nerve gas.

THE TWELVE YEARS OF SANCTIONS ON IRAQ LED to feelings of mistrust and antagonism between the West and the Middle East. Although the Arabs were well aware of the disgraceful acts of Saddam Hussein, they did not see why the Iraqi people should suffer for his crimes. The confrontation between Iraq and the world community, the latter headed by the United States, became a further grievance in the eyes of many Arab people. It ranked alongside the Israeli occupation of Palestinian land in the West Bank and Gaza Strip. Some Arab people believe that this Israeli occupation is supported by the United States, and have come to regard the United States as their enemy.

Islamic Fundamentalism

Throughout the Islamic world, religious leaders promoting fundamentalist views have been hugely successful. Such leaders want to reject all compromise between Islam and the West. According to fundamentalists, all aspects of life must be entirely governed by the Sunna, that is to say the Koran, the Muslim holy book, together with the traditionally accepted written records of what the Prophet Muhammad did and said in his lifetime.

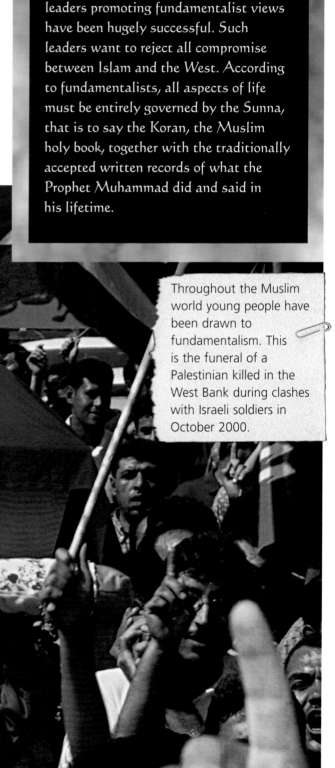

Throughout the Muslim world young people have been drawn to fundamentalism. This is the funeral of a Palestinian killed in the West Bank during clashes with Israeli soldiers in October 2000.

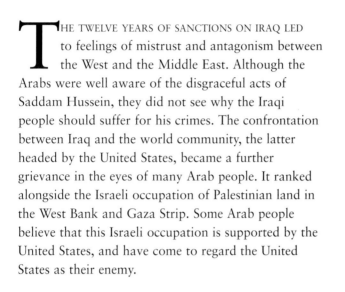

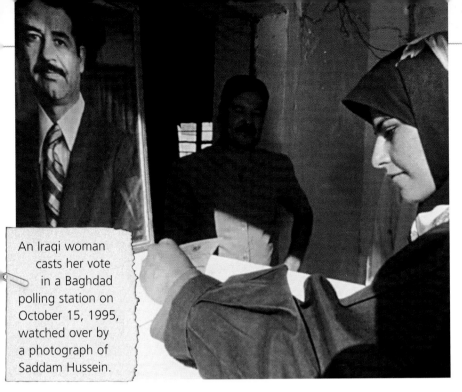

An Iraqi woman casts her vote in a Baghdad polling station on October 15, 1995, watched over by a photograph of Saddam Hussein.

The occupation of Iraq by the U.S. and allied forces in April 2003 changed the situation in the Middle East. Many Arab countries were glad to see Saddam go. But they were not convinced that the government of an Arab state, no matter how bad, should be overthrown by a Western invasion. Popular unrest remained a possibility. Concern is also felt by the conservative monarchies of the Gulf (Kuwait, Bahrain, Qatar, the United Arab Emirates, Oman, and Saudi Arabia) and by Arab states such as Jordan and Egypt, which are friendly with the United States and Britain. The Gulf War was one reason for the rise in support for Muslim fundamentalism. The invasion of Iraq seemed likely to increase this support. Violence in the name of Islam appears to be increasingly acceptable to some fundamentalist groups.

There seemed no doubt, until the United States began to step up the pressure to a high level in the early months of 2003, that Saddam Hussein was still trying to maintain his armed forces. It also appeared that he might still have nonconventional weapons.

The Media and the War

Throughout the years of confrontation between the West and Iraq, the role of the media has been extremely important. The Gulf War received wide television coverage, though paradoxically there was little direct reporting of actual fighting on the ground. However, during the war both the West and Iraq strictly controlled access by the media. The allied leaders allowed the reporters and cameras to see only what was beneficial to them. In 2003, the allied forces gave journalists on the ground more access. Iraq also allowed journalists to cover the war. During the Gulf War, Iraq had carefully controlled what journalists saw and whom they met. The same was true in 2003, until the Iraqi government collapsed.

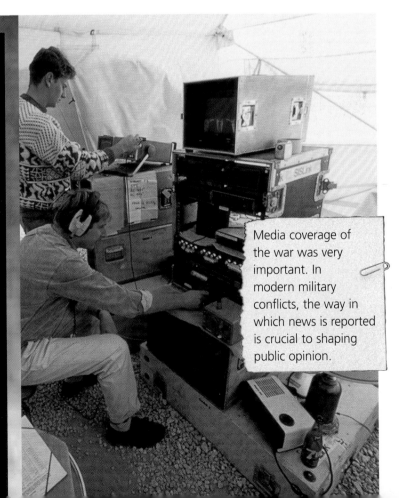

Media coverage of the war was very important. In modern military conflicts, the way in which news is reported is crucial to shaping public opinion.

41

ON SEPTEMBER 11, 2001, ISLAMIC fundamentalist terrorists gained control of two U.S. passenger planes and flew them into the twin towers of the World Trade Center in New York City. As a result, thousands of civilians were killed. Another aircraft was crashed into the Pentagon, the headquarters of the United States Department of Defense, and a fourth aircraft crashed in Pennsylvania. The terrorist attacks were believed to have been carried out by members of the Al-Qaeda terrorist network. In response, President George W. Bush declared a "war on terrorism." This first took the shape of a U.S.-led attack on Afghanistan. Its goal was to destroy the regime of the Taliban and fundamentalist leader Osama Bin Laden's terrorist organization Al-Qaeda, which the Taliban was said to be harboring.

Since the summer of 2002, President Bush made it clear that he was considering an armed attack on Iraq with the objective of ousting Saddam Hussein. United Nations weapons inspectors began work again in November 2002, after UN Security Council Resolution 1441 was passed. The Bush administration said it believed Iraq possessed chemical and biological weapons that were a threat to world peace, and that Iraq had not abandoned its attempts to build a nuclear bomb.

The United Nations weapons inspectors failed to find indisputable evidence of Iraqi wrongdoing. Their report in January 2003 did not clear Saddam Hussein, but was not enough to lead to an immediate attack on Iraq. In the spring of 2003, the United States tried get the Security Council to pass another resolution that would be a justification to attack Iraq in order to, as President Bush put it, "disarm Iraq by force." Other nations that were members of the Security Council refused to back the American plan. In

President George W. Bush insisted from the beginning that he had the right to attack Iraq.

A Threat to World Peace

" Once again, this nation and our friends are all that stand between a world at peace, and a world of chaos and constant alarm. Once again, we are called to defend the safety of our people, and the hopes of all mankind. And we accept this responsibility. America is making a broad and determined effort to confront these dangers. We have called on the United Nations to fulfill its charter, and stand by its demand that Iraq disarm. "

President George W. Bush, January 29, 2003

U.S. troops enter Baghdad on April 9, 2003. The city was filled with images of Saddam Hussein, like the one pictured here.

particular France and Russia—which as permanent members of the Council have the right to veto any resolution—said they would block any U.S. attempt to get the United Nations' backing for an assault on Iraq.

President Bush therefore decided to act alone. On March 20, together with forces from Britain and a handful of troops from Australia, the United States attacked Iraq. The war lasted just three weeks. On April 9, American troops entered Baghdad, and by April 12 the victory appeared total. By that time 163 allied soldiers had been killed. Several thousand Iraqi civilians lost their lives, as well as many thousands of Iraqi troops.

Iraq's future in the spring of 2003 appeared uncertain. The vast majority of the Iraqi people seemed happy to see Saddam go, but were not enthusiastic about the presence of American troops. The United States set up a military administration, and appeared determined to install an Iraqi democratic government. Newly stirring political forces in Iraq, especially among the Shi'a population and the Kurds, seemed to have other ideas. Iraq's Arab neighbors, as well as Turkey and Iran, watched developments with concern. The future of Iraq was hard to predict, but there would clearly be consequences for the Middle East as a whole and for the relationship between the United States and the world's Arab and Muslim peoples.

43

Glossary

alliance group of countries that cooperate in a military operation. They are often known as "allies" and are said to be "allied" to each other.

Allied Powers countries that fought against Germany during World War I. The alliance was led by Britain, France, and the United States.

Al-Qaeda network anti-Western Muslim fundamentalist organization led by Osama bin Laden and originally based in Afghanistan. Al-Qaeda is believed to be responsible for the attack that destroyed the World Trade Center on September 11, 2001. The network also appears to have been involved in a number of other terrorist attacks around the world.

Arab League political organization set up by the Arab states in 1945, to which all Arab countries now belong

Baath Party secular (nonreligious) Arab nationalist party founded in Syria in the 1930s

coalition group of countries, armies, or political parties acting together

conscript person who is required to join an army. In many countries young men are conscripted into the army at a particular age, usually 18. Women are not usually conscripted, except in Israel.

dictator ruler who governs his country alone, with the power to make all decisions without consulting any other person or institution, such as a parliament. A country ruled by a dictator is known as a dictatorship.

diplomacy/diplomatic relations the practice of relations between states, usually carried out by professionals called diplomats. When two countries exchange ambassadors, they are said to have diplomatic relations. This implies that they recognize each other's government.

fundamentalism form of religious belief that insists on returning to the so-called "fundamentals," which are what the original scriptures or prophet has laid down, with no later interpretation

guerrilla irregular soldier, who fights individually with hit-and-run tactics rather than in an army

Gulf Cooperation Council organization set up in 1981 by Saudi Arabia, Kuwait, Qatar, Bahrain, the United Arab Emirates, and Oman as a joint defense organization. It now has a large political and economic role.

Kurds inhabitants of northern Iraq, southeastern Turkey, and some adjacent areas. Kurds speak a language of their own that is related to Persian, not Arabic. They are mostly Sunni Muslims, with some Shi'ites and other sects.

mandate formal order. At the end of World War I, the new international body, the League of Nations, awarded mandates to Britain and France to govern Middle Eastern countries that were formerly part of the Ottoman Empire.

militant person prepared to take vigorous and sometimes violent action on behalf of a principle in which he or she believes

military coup taking over of the government of a country by the armed forces

Muslim follower of Islam

Muslim fundamentalists Muslims who wish to return to the basic principles of Islam as they see them

nationalist person who feels strongly about acting in the best interests of his or her nation

neutral/neutrality country that does not take sides or form alliances in international conflicts or wars. Switzerland is a traditionally neutral country. In any given situation, it is open to particular countries to remain neutral. Neutral countries are said to maintain neutrality.

nonconventional weapons chemical, biological, and nuclear weapons, also sometimes called Weapons of Mass Destruction (WMD)

occupied territories territories, formerly part of the territory of Palestine, that did not become part of Israel in 1948, and that Israel occupied in 1967

OPEC (Organization of Petroleum Exporting Countries) group of some of the oil-exporting countries, including Kuwait and Saudi Arabia, that has its headquarters in Vienna and holds regular meetings to make decisions about oil production and prices

Ottoman Empire Turkish-ruled state whose capital was in Istanbul, and that governed most of the Middle East before World War I. Most of the Arab countries were part of the Ottoman Empire, including Iraq and Kuwait, though the level of political control that the Ottoman Empire was able to exert varied widely.

PLO (Palestine Liberation Organization) organization set up by Palestinian exiles in 1964 to struggle for independence and political recognition for the Palestinians, whose land became part of Israel in 1948. Israel took control of the remaining Palestinian lands in the West Bank and Gaza in 1967.

rationing government-ordered limits on the distribution of food or any other commodity to make sure there is enough for everyone in the country

regime another word for government, but implying that the particular government's right to rule may not be regarded by everyone as legitimate

religious minorities groups of people in a country whose religion is different from that of the majority

republic political system that is governed by a president and an elected assembly

sanctions measures imposed against a country that are intended to change that country's policy by causing economic hardship. For example, trade may be banned, or travel forbidden.

Scud missiles missiles originally manufactured in the Soviet Union and used by Iraq during the Gulf War against Israel and Saudi Arabia

secretary of state senior official in the U.S. administration who, under the president's direction, controls U.S. relations with other countries

Security Council body at the United Nations that monitors crisis situations and issues resolutions that members of the UN must obey. It has five permanent members (the United States, Britain, France, Russia, and China) and ten temporary members drawn from the membership of the UN.

Shi'a/Shi'ite Muslims Muslim minority who have some traditions and beliefs that differ slightly from the Sunni Muslim tradition. They believe that the leadership of Islam descended through the Prophet Muhammad's cousin and son-in-law Ali. Ten percent of the world's Muslims are Shi'ites, and they live mainly in Iran, which is almost entirely Shi'ite.

smart bomb weapon that is electronically guided or guides itself with great accuracy to hit its target

Sunna the Koran and the tradition of the prophet Muhammad's life, on which Islam and Islamic law and observance are based

Sunni Muslims Muslims who base their faith on the Sunna. Ninety percent of the world's billion Muslims are Sunni.

United Nations (UN) world forum and discussion body set up in 1945 after World War II, with the goal of maintaining world peace

West Bank part of Palestine adjacent to the Jordan River that Israel did not annex in the Arab-Israeli war of 1948. The West Bank was annexed by Jordan, but was occupied by Israel in 1967, together with the Gaza Strip in southwest Israel on the Mediterranean, which had previously been administered by Egypt.

Further Reading

Cockburn, Andrew and Patrick Cockburn. *Out of the Ashes: The Resurrection of Saddam Hussein.* Collingdale, Penn.: DIANE, 2001.

Hossell, Karen Price. *20th Century History Makers: The Persian Gulf War.* Chicago: Heinemann, 2003.

Newell, Clayton R. *Historical Dictionary of the Persian Gulf War, 1990–1991.* Lanham, Md.: Scarecrow Press, 1998.

Tripp, Charles. *A History of Iraq.* New York: Cambridge University Press, 2002.

Timeline

April 28, 1937 Saddam Hussein is born in the village of Shawish near Tikrit in central Iraq.

October 7, 1959 Saddam takes part in a failed plot against President Qassem and flees the country. Becomes a student in Cairo.

February 8, 1963 President Qassem is assassinated. Saddam Hussein returns to Iraq.

July 17, 1968 President Bakr (a cousin of Saddam's father) takes power. Saddam becomes vice president of the Revolutionary Command Council.

March 20, 1973 Iraq seizes the Kuwaiti border post at Samita and Kuwaiti and Iraqi troops exchange fire.

July 16, 1979 Saddam Hussein becomes president of Iraq.

September 22, 1980 Saddam launches Iraq's attack on Iran.

March 28, 1988 Saddam Hussein uses chemical weapons against Iraqi Kurds at Halabja.

August 20, 1988 A ceasefire is declared between Iraq and Iran at Iraq's request.

February 16, 1989 Saddam Hussein takes Iraq into the Arab Cooperation Council with Egypt, Jordan, and Yemen.

July 17, 1990 Saddam threatens Kuwait.

July 25, 1990 Saddam meets with U.S. ambassador April Glaspie.

July 31, 1990 Negotiations in Saudi Arabia between Iraq and Kuwait fail.

August 2, 1990 (Kuwait time) Iraqi forces invade Kuwait.

November 29, 1990 The UN passes Resolution 687, sets January 15 as a deadline for Iraqi withdrawal from Kuwait.

January 15, 1991 The UN deadline passes with no response from Iraq.

January 17, 1991 (Kuwait time) Allied air attack on Iraq and Iraqi army in Kuwait begins.

February 14, 1991 (Kuwait time) Land attack on Iraq's occupying forces begins.

February 28, 1991 Fighting ends.

March 3, 1991 Iraq surrenders.

April 3, 1991 The ceasefire under UN Resolution 687 is adopted.

June 9, 1991 UNSCOM (United Nations Special Commission) arms inspectors arrive for the first time in Iraq.

December 9, 1996 UN Secretary General Boutros Boutros-Ghali gives final approval to a long-delayed "oil for food" deal, which allows Iraq to export a limited amount of oil for the first time since its invasion of Kuwait. UN resolutions permitting this were passed in 1995.

December 16, 1998 UNSCOM weapons inspectors are withdrawn for the last time, after Iraqi noncooperation.

December 17, 1998 The U.S. orders the start of the air war, known as "Operation Desert Fox." President Clinton orders an extensive air attack on Iraqi military facilities.

January 29, 2002 President George W. Bush condemns Iraq, Iran, and North Korea for seeking weapons of mass destruction and sponsoring terrorism.

November 2002 UN weapons inspectors return to Iraq.

January 29, 2003 President Bush calls upon the UN to stand by its demand that Iraq disarm.

March 20, 2003 U.S., British, and Australian forces invade Iraq.

April 9, 2003 Allied forces enter Baghdad.

August 2, 1990: the Iraqi military invades Kuwait.

Index